SHEEP HUNTING

A TO Z

A 26-POINT GUIDE
TO SUCCESSFUL SHEEP
HUNTING

Bill Rose

This book is dedicated to my dad, Jack W. Rose.
Thanks for taking me on that first hunt.
Who would have ever thought it would
become such a passion for me.
Love and miss you, Dad!

TABLE OF CONTENTS

Forward   i

1. PREPARATION   1

    a. Emotional, Physical, and Mental   1

    b. Training Regimens   3

    c. Shoot Your Rifle – A Lot!   5

    d. Learning about Sheep   7

    e. DIY or Guided?   9

2. EQUIPMENT   11

    f. Clothing   11

    g. Footwear   13

    h. Rifles and Ammunition   15

    i. Optics   17

    j. Packs and Pack Frames   20

    k. Hiking Gear   22

    l. Survival Gear   24

    m. Orienteering   27

    n. Communications Equipment   29

    o. Camping and Miscellaneous Equipment   31

3. HYDRATION AND NUTRITION   33

    p. Water and Hydration   33

    q. Food   35

4. SHEEP STEW   37

    r. Miscellaneous Suggestions and Ideas   37

TABLE OF CONTENTS

5. PRE-HUNT   39

    s. Pre-Season Activities   39

6. THE HUNT   43

    t. Locating the Sheep   43

    u. The Stalk   44

    v. Making the Shot   46

    w. Picture Time!   48

    x. The Real Work Begins   50

7. POST- HUNT   53

    y. Caring for Your Trophy and Meat   53

    z. What Now?   55

COMPANY/PRODUCT ENDORSEMENTS   58

SUMMARY   61

FORWARD

In May of 2000, I received notification that I had drawn my first bighorn sheep tag in Colorado. I immediately called some of my hunting buddies and told them of my good fortune. After congratulating me, one of my friends warned me that I was about to catch what he called "sheep fever". At the time, I really didn't understand what he was talking about. Five months later, after ten scouting trips, countless hours of shooting and preparation, nine days of hunting, and failing by the smallest of margins to harvest a bighorn sheep, I understood. I was hopelessly hooked on sheep hunting.

Six years later, I drew another sheep tag in Colorado. This time, I finished the job and took my first bighorn sheep with Joe Boucher of Horn Fork Guides. It was the highlight of my hunting life and it will be the highlight of yours too, if you are lucky enough to harvest one of these incredible animals.

This book is the result of my passion for sheep hunting as well as a desire to help others succeed in this great sporting activity. This book is simple and concise. It is not an "all-inclusive" resource for sheep hunting. I have simply shared some of what I have learned through participating in two sheep hunts myself. It is my hope that the information found in this book will not only help you to prepare for your hunt, but it will provide some of the tools necessary for you to take a sheep.

Good luck and happy hunting!

Bill Rose

1. PREPARATION

a. **EMOTIONAL PREPARATION**   Hunting sheep is much the same as hunting other big game species. They can be very difficult to locate and at times, it can be very disheartening.   Add in terrain that is steep and rocky, weather conditions that can be downright nasty, a few blown attempts at a stalk, and you have the makings of some pretty discouraging moments.

A sheep hunter must maintain a "never give up" attitude. Remember, in the hunting game, your luck can change in a flash. I hunted for eight days during my first sheep hunt before I even saw a bighorn sheep. And then, I only saw him long enough for me to get my safety off, my rifle up to my shoulder, just in time to watch him wheel around and disappear behind some evergreen trees. I didn't even get the shot off and I never saw him again.

During my second sheep hunt, it was the last day of the hunt. We had ridden horses in about five miles to a place where one of my outfitter's guides had seen several rams the day before. We got there only to find a bunch of ewes and lambs. Not giving in to the situation, my outfitter suggested we move to another ridge to see if we could locate the rams. As we were riding down the trail towards that ridge I remember thinking to myself, "You're going home without a sheep. Did you enjoy this expensive camping trip?" Little did I know three hours later I would be standing over my first bighorn sheep. And it all happened because my outfitter refused to quit.

I will never forget the voice inside my head repeatedly saying to me as we climbed that last ridge, "Don't you quit! Don't you quit!" I am so glad we didn't give up. Taking that ram was one of the all-time biggest thrills of my life!

PHYSICAL PREPARATION   Sheep hunting is one of the most physically taxing hunts you will ever experience. If you are going to endure the rigors of a sheep hunt, you must train, and train hard. I recommend you begin your training regimen at least four months in advance of your hunt. I also recommend that you get a physical examination by your doctor prior to beginning your training. If you are overweight, I suggest that you set a goal to lose some weight. I lost 15 pounds before my second sheep hunt and it helped me tremendously in navigating the mountains I hunted. Remember, every pound you lose is one less pound you have to drag up that mountain. Your feet and legs will thank you.

MENTAL PREPARATION   As I stated earlier, there are many potential challenges you will face while on your sheep hunt. One of those challenges is fatigue, both physical and mental. The physical fatigue that you will experience will affect your ability to think and react properly. I recommend that you practice in your mind, situations that may occur. What will you do if a sheep appears out of nowhere? Will you take a snap shot? Are you comfortable doing so and are you a skilled enough marksman to be able to make a clean kill without wounding and possibly losing the animal? Mental focus will be a key element to filling your tag.

Remember, there is no celebrating until the animal is on the ground, and to get it there requires that you be able to remain calm as you make the shot. Practicing in your mind how you will react in different situations, and under different conditions, will aid you executing the shot properly.

b.

TRAINING REGIMEN On a sheep hunt, the terrain where you will be hunting will, for the most part, be steep and rocky. It will involve a lot of hiking and you will most likely cover many miles. In order for you to enjoy your hunt, it is important that you be in the best physical condition possible.

Before my first sheep hunt, I found a training regimen on line that I used to get into shape that was simple and very effective. It involves finding a hill that you can walk up and down in a total of 6-8 minutes. It does not matter how steep the hill is, just that you can complete the round trip up and back down in 6-8 minutes. For me, it just so happened that I had such a hill about a mile from my house. It was about a quarter mile in length and I found that I could walk up and back down in 7 minutes. Two round trips gave me a mile walk and I started out doing two miles per day, three days per week. I worked my way up to the point that I was doing six miles per day, three to four days per week. On the other two days, I lifted weights and rode my bicycle 4-5 miles. I took Sundays off to recuperate. I found that this regimen worked well for me.

There are, however, two things for which I have found it difficult to train. One is the altitude at which you will be hunting. Sheep live at elevations of 6000 feet and above, and the higher the elevation, the less oxygen there will be in the air. Less oxygen translates into shortness of breath and greater physical fatigue. Regardless of the type or amount of training you do, it is impossible to recreate the effect thin air will have on your lungs and your body, especially if you live at or near sea level.

The best way to deal with the challenge of altitude is to arrive at your hunting area a couple of days in advance. Hiking and scouting during those two days will allow your body to acclimate. If early arrival is not possible, realize that breathing will be more difficult during your first couple of days of the hunt until your body gets used to the lack of oxygen. If you are lucky enough to live in a state where there are mountains like I do, you could train by hiking in those mountains. In Colorado, we have 53 peaks that are 14,000 feet or higher. Hiking one or two of those peaks in advance of your hunt will help you to adjust to the altitude you will experience during your hunt. A word of caution…learn the signs of altitude sickness and be aware of how you are feeling while hiking at high altitude during your training, and in particular, during the first few days of your hunt. If you experience the symptoms of altitude sickness, get off of the mountain and if need be, get help.

The other difficult thing to train for is the effect walking on steep, rocky, mountain sides will have on your legs. When I was younger, I would train hard for my deer and elk hunts. I would walk stairs. I would sidestep the stairs and I was still sore after the first few days of the hunt. It was the side-hill walking that was making me sore. I have learned to combat this by actually training on side hills. I suggest that you find a steep hill that you can repeatedly walk along to get your legs in shape. I also suggest that you find a location that is rocky to walk on to prepare your legs and feet for the rocky terrain that you will be hunting in during your sheep hunt. I suggest you wear the hunting boots you will be using during your hunt so that you can both acclimate your feet to your boots, as well as provide the added ankle support you will need to train on the side-hill and on the rocky terrain. Whatever you do, take care not to sprain an ankle or a knee during your training.

C. **SHOOT YOUR RIFLE-A LOT!** I cannot stress enough how important it is that you practice shooting your rifle. You have probably waited for years to draw that coveted sheep tag you now hold, and the only way to fill it is by utilizing your shooting skills. I suggest you shoot at least two boxes of ammunition a week in advance of your hunt. There are several reasons for doing so.

By practicing this much, you will become intimately familiar with your rifle and what it feels like when you fire it. You will become used to the recoil, and the more comfortable you are with the recoil, the better your aim will be. You will get a better feel for the amount of pressure required to pull the trigger. Again, greater familiarity with your trigger will result in better accuracy in your shots.

I suggest you practice shooting from a variety of different positions including, lying down prone, sitting, standing, and from a rest. If you will be carrying shooting sticks during your hunt (and I strongly suggest that you do), shoot off of the shooting sticks from different positions. Practicing shooting from different positions will help you prepare for any scenario that may occur during your hunt and will better improve your chances of making the shot, no matter the circumstances.

If you are lucky enough to live in a place where there are hills that you can set up targets above and below your shooting point, do it! The chances are very high that when you get a shot at a sheep in the field, it will not be at an elevation that is level with where you are standing. So any practice that you can do that involves shooting up or downhill will be to your advantage. Remember, bullet drop is only affected by the horizontal distance to your target. So in most cases, you will hold right on or a little low when shooting up or downhill.

If you are able to practice shooting at moving targets, I strongly suggest that you take advantage of that opportunity, also. I know of a hunter who places cardboard disks inside of old automobile tires, rolls them off of hills, and then tries to hit the disk as they bounce down the side of the hill. If you are able to do the same thing, and

5

can get proficient at hitting those moving targets, you will have no problem in harvesting a sheep, should the opportunity present itself.

Finally, a word to the wise. No matter how much you shoot in advance of your hunt, make sure you check every mounting screw in your rifle prior to going into the field. I was on my first sheep hunt and it was the second day of the hunt. My son, my nephew and I had climbed about a thousand feet straight up a mountainside right at first light. The terrain was very rocky and steep and it took us almost four hours to complete the climb. We found a good spot to be able to see into a high basin and sat down to rest and watch for a while. As I sat there holding my rifle, I had my thumb over the top of the stock and my index finger around the outside of the trigger guard. I happened to squeeze my hand a little bit as I shifted sitting positions and felt movement between the trigger guard and the stock. Upon examination of my rifle, I discovered that both screws on either side of the trigger guard were loose. I took out my Leatherman and tightened them, but I knew it would be very risky to take a shot at an animal having had that much play in the mounting. Fortunately, we saw no sheep that morning and shortly thereafter, a thunderstorm drove us off of the mountain. Upon returning home the next day, I tightened all of the mounting screws in my stock and took the rifle out to the range to test fire it. On my first shot, I was six inches to the left at 50 yards! I definitely learned a lesson about thoroughly checking my rifle before going into the field!

d. **LEARNING ABOUT SHEEP** Having a thorough understanding about the animal you will be hunting is a key element to returning home successful. There are several things you can do to increase your understanding about bighorn sheep. You've taken the first step by reading this book. I suggest you read as many books about bighorn sheep as possible, prior to the start of your hunt. A few titles that come to mind are listed below:

"Wild Sheep Country" by Valerius Geist

"The Art of Hunting Big Game in North America" by Jack O'Connor

"Montana-Land of Giant Rams" and "Quest for Dall Rams" by Duncan Gilchrist

"Sheep Hunting in Alaska" by Tony Russ

These books and many others about sheep hunting can be purchased online at www.wildramhunters.net.

I also suggest that you watch as many sheep hunting videos as possible. Viewing videos is a great way to learn about sheep and their habitat. You will also be able to get an idea of the great adventure you are about to embark on. A few of my favorite sheep hunting videos are listed below:

"Full Curl - Hunting the Canadian Wilderness" by Bart Lancaster

"Hunt'n Rams – The Guide's Eye" by Bart Lancaster

"Black Shale White Sheep" by Timberline Video Productions

The videos listed here are generally available at Sportsman's Warehouse. There are a number of other great videos on sheep hunting that are available at www.wildramhunters.net.

I also suggest that you create a scrapbook of bighorn sheep pictures. You can derive these pictures from magazine publications such as "Eastman's Hunting Journal" and "The Huntin'Fool" magazine from Carter Hunter Services. Eastman's devotes one entire issue per year to sheep hunting. If you see a picture of a sheep, cut it out and put it in your scrapbook. Spend a significant amount of time studying the scrapbook. It will help you familiarize yourself with sheep horns and how they look from all different angles. It will also help you to practice field judging them.

I also suggest you learn as much as you can about how sheep react to hunting pressure. Talk to as many sheep hunters as possible, especially those that have hunted in the area you have drawn. If possible, take them to lunch and pay for their meal. Also, call the wildlife biologist in the state you will be hunting, to learn what he/she has to say about your hunting area as well as the habits of the sheep in the area. Record any tips you get in a hunting journal and review the information repeatedly to impress it in your mind.

Here are a couple of tips I learned from my two sheep hunts. Sheep have very good eyes and noses. Their hearing is good as is most big game animal's, but their ears are small, so they are not going to respond to what they hear like a mule deer will. Because they live in an environment where there are a lot of loose rocks, they have a tendency, for the most part, to ignore rolling rocks. Like most big game animals, they operate on the 66% premise. That is, anytime they have been alerted by two out of their three senses, they are going to flee. Sheep are best approached from above. I must admit that I have read the opposite also, that is, that they are best approached from below. But both my outfitter, on my second sheep hunt, and I have found this not to be the case. They rarely look up and approaching them from above is definitely going to be to your advantage.

DO-IT-YOURSELF OR GUIDED? You've spent years waiting to draw that coveted sheep tag. Now what do you do? Do you spend the money and hunt with an outfitter, or do you head out on your own to and do it yourself? I've done both and I have to say there are advantages to both options.

I drew my first sheep tag in 2000. It took me six years to draw the tag and I was fully motivated to fill it. I was contacted by a local outfitter who was licensed in the area in which I had drawn my tag. It would cost $5000 to have him guide me. I wanted to accept his offer, but I just didn't have the money at the time. So I set about to make the hunt happen on my own. I worked hard at it. I made ten trips to my area to scout for sheep. Fortunately, my area was only an hour and a half from my home, so it was doable for me. I only saw sheep on two of those scouting trips, but it gave me hope that I could pull the hunt off on my own.

I hunted for nine days, but not concurrently. Because the area was relatively close to my home, I would hunt for a day and then return home to rest for a day. I hunted alone for six of the nine days. I didn't see a ram until the eighth day I hunted, and as I described in the Forward, I jumped him out of his bed and he eluded me before I could squeeze the trigger. I saw two rams on the last day of the season, but it was late in the day and I was not able to get into position to take a shot before the sun went down on that evening and on my hunt. I was devastated that I had not filled my tag.

Six years later in 2006, I drew another sheep tag. It was in a different area farther from my home, so scouting was going to be more difficult. I felt it could very well be my last chance to draw a sheep tag, so after discussing it with my wife, I decided it would be best for me to hire an outfitter. It made all the difference in the world as I ended up taking my first bighorn sheep. Don't get me wrong, hiring an outfitter was not the only reason I was able to fill my tag. There are lots of sheep hunters who harvest sheep every year on "do-it-yourself" hunts. But after hunting with an outfitter I came to the conclusion that it does have its advantages, if you can afford it. The chart on the next page outlines the differences.

DO-IT-YOURSELF	HIRE AN OUTFITTER
Cost: Whatever you decide	Cost: $5000 and up
Scouting will be up to you.	Scouting will be done in advance by the outfitter and his guides.
You provide and cook your own food.	Food and cooking are provided.
You provide the tent and all equipment necessary to camp.	Tent and all necessary camping equipment will be provided with exception of your personal items (sleeping bag, pillow, cot, etc.)
You provide all optics including spotting scope.	Spotting scope provided. Bring your own binoculars (your spotting scope is optional)
You provide means to access area – ATV's, truck, rental of horses, tack, etc.	ATV's, trucks, horses, tack, etc. provided
You arrange for a hunting companion.	Hunting companionship provided by your guide.
Whatever experience you have hunting sheep is what you will have to rely upon.	Tap into hundreds, if not thousands of hours of sheep hunting experience. (This is invaluable!)
If you shoot a sheep, you field dress it, pack it, and care for the meat, head, hide, etc.	If you shoot a sheep, there will be multiple individuals available to help with the field dressing, packing, and care for the meat, head, hide, etc.

2. EQUIPMENT

f. **CLOTHING**   For the most part, the clothing you will need to sheep hunt is the same as what you would use to participate in any other type of big game hunting. You will want to dress in layers as the climate found in high altitude hunting, can be both mild and unforgiving all in the same day. It is not uncommon to experience all four of the seasons during a sheep hunt, so you have to be prepared.

RULE #1   Prior to my last sheep hunt, my outfitter advised me that under no circumstance was I to bring any clothing made of cotton on the hunt. I encourage you to follow this rule.

BASE LAYERS   Your base layer should be a polyester-based material with moisture-wicking, fast drying capability. I suggest you utilize the scent-blocking technology that is available in today's clothing, also. Your long underwear should also have moisture-wicking capability. If you will be hunting during a late season where snow will be more prevalent, I suggest you bring at least one pair of wool blend long underwear.

OUTER LAYERS   I suggest that all of your outer clothing, including shirts, pants, vests, jackets and coats have some kind of camouflage pattern. I prefer those with lighter color variations, since much of the terrain you can find yourself hunting in, is above timberline where there are no trees and even less shadows. My experience is that the darker colors found in many of the camo patterns tend to blend together, making your silhouette much more visible when you are out in the open. Fortunately in recent years, there have been a number of new patterns with lighter color variations that have been introduced into the marketplace, which I believe will be much more advantageous to a sheep hunter.

RAINGEAR   The most important article of clothing you will possess on a sheep hunt will be your raingear. Whatever you do, make sure you buy the best raingear you can afford. I suggest raingear with Gore-Tex® or one of the similar products on the market today. It should be lightweight, breathable and packable, as it will be something you will carry in your backpack. I learned this lesson on my first sheep hunt. It rained on six of the nine days I hunted. By the third day my nylon raingear was soaked and had lost its ability to shed water. As a result, I got wet and that made for some uncomfortable hunting. Prior to my second sheep hunt I purchased quality raingear. It cost me $250, but it was worth it. I have since used that raingear on multiple hunts of all types and have never gotten wet, regardless of the weather conditions. It has also proven itself to be a great extra layer that is wind-proof. Spend the money to purchase quality raingear. You will be glad you did!

HEADWEAR   You will want to bring headwear for a variety of weather conditions. I prefer a baseball-style cap for most hunting situations. I suggest you refrain from the use of large brimmed hats such as cowboy hats, as the winds at high altitude will make it difficult to keep it on your head. Cold weather conditions will require that you have a stocking cap or head sock to keep your ears warm. I really like the new lightweight skull caps and face masks that have recently been introduced. They work well and fit nicely in your pocket when you aren't wearing them. They come in a variety of camo patterns, which is also nice.

RULE #2   Make sure that your clothing fits properly, is comfortable, breathable, and will warm you adequately. Doing so will ensure you have an enjoyable hunt.

g. **FOOTWEAR**   Your feet will play a major role in helping you to accomplish your goal of harvesting a sheep. It is a given they will become tired and sore from hiking. The challenge is to keep them warm, dry, and ultimately, comfortable. That means your footwear has to be insulated, waterproof and of the best quality you can afford.

SOCKS   To guard against blisters, you will want to wear two pairs of socks with your hunting boots. A lightweight polypropylene sock should be worn under a thicker, wool blend hunting sock.   The lightweight sock will wick moisture away from your skin, which will keep your feet dry. It will also help prevent blisters, should your foot move inside your boot. The wool blend sock will keep your feet warm, even if they get wet. I suggest you bring a set of socks for every day you will be hunting and that you make sure you wear a clean set daily. This will ensure you begin the day with dry feet, a must for comfort and blister prevention.

BOOTS   I suggest that you buy a new set of boots for your sheep hunt, as you will want to have lugged soles that are fresh with maximum gripping power. You will be hiking in steep, rocky terrain and you will want to have the best grip available. Make sure you get boots that lace well up your legs to provide adequate ankle support.

When you purchase your boots, choose boots with an insulation value compatible with the temperature and weather conditions that could be expected during the time of the year you will be hunting. An early season hunt in August or September will most likely be warmer than a late season hunt in October or November. My suggestion would be to buy boots with 500-750 grams of Thinsulate® for an early season hunt, and 1000-1200 grams of Thinsulate® for a late season hunt. Since each person has different circulation in their legs and feet, and a different tolerance for cold, adjust according to your personal requirements.

Your boots must be waterproof and breathable. Regardless whether you will be hunting an early or late season, you will undoubtedly experience some kind of precipitation during the hunt. Whether it is rain or snow, your feet must remain dry if you are to be able to hunt comfortably. Your boots should be equipped with Gore-Tex® or some other compatible waterproofing material that is breathable and will allow your boots to work in conjunction with your socks.

Along with being insulated and waterproof, your boots need to be lightweight. Keep in mind that every ounce of weight in your boots is an ounce of weight that your legs will be lifting for every step you take. Considering that you will be hiking a lot of miles, and thousands of feet of elevation change during your hunt, you will be well served to minimize the number of ounces of weight you will be carrying, including those in your boots.

INSOLES   Finally, prior to my second sheep hunt, my outfitter suggested that I remove the factory insoles that came in my boots and replace them with insoles that would provide stiffer support for my feet. He suggested it because of the rocky terrain we would be hunting. I did so and the difference was remarkable. My feet got tired from all of the walking, but they felt better at the end of the day and seemed to recover quicker. I highly recommend replacing the insoles of your boots. You can find the replacement insoles at any quality outdoor sporting goods store.

h.

RIFLES AND AMMUNITION Most any caliber rifle you would typically use to hunt big game will work for sheep hunting. However, it should be noted that sheep are fairly large animals, and to make sure that the animal goes down on the first shot, you will want to utilize a rifle caliber that is on the heavier side or powered by a magnum load. A flat shooting rifle such as a .270 or .280 will certainly work, but I prefer those calibers in the magnum load for better effectiveness. The .300 magnum or .300 short magnum are also great loads for sheep. I shoot a Browning® BBR chambered in the Rem 7MM magnum caliber and it absolutely did the job when I harvested my sheep.

As with every other piece of equipment you will be packing up the mountain, you want your rifle to be as light as possible. For every pound you save in weight, it's one less pound you have to carry up and back down the mountain. That said, there are some wonderful ultra light rifles available now that can help with this challenge. The downside to them is the lighter the rifle, the more recoil it can produce. So if you choose to utilize an ultra light, make sure you shoot it enough in advance to get comfortable with the recoil.

I suggest you choose a rifle with a composite stock. While I love the look of a wood stock, they tend to be much heavier than a composite stock and they are definitely more susceptible to scratches and scrapes from the rocks you will experience in sheep country.

You will also want to choose a rifle with matte bluing to prevent the glint that can come from a rifle barrel that has standard bluing.

A quality sling is a must for your rifle. It will help to eliminate arm and hand fatigue and provide a way for you to keep your hands free as you hike and climb. This will be of tremendous value to you during the course of your hunt.

Regardless of the features of your rifle, the most important consideration of all will be your familiarity and level of comfort you have with your rifle. You can have the lightest, most sturdy and reliable rifle ever, but if you cannot hit anything when you shoot it, you will not fill your tag. You have to be able to shoot without worrying about the recoil, if you are going to be accurate. As I stated earlier in this book, you will want to practice shooting as much as possible to increase your familiarity with your rifle as well as increase your confidence as a marksman. This will markedly increase your odds of taking a sheep.

AMMUNITION Hunters often discount the importance ammunition plays in their hunting success. In my opinion, the better the quality of your ammunition, the better you will shoot. I am a believer in loading your own ammunition. It will help you learn the intricacies of your rifle, as well as develop a load that will far exceed the accuracy of any factory load you could purchase. Case in point, I used to own a Remington 30.06 rifle that I have since passed on to my oldest son. While I owned it, I developed a load for that rifle which was remarkable. There were numerous occasions while shooting the load, where I shot through the hole in the target made by the previous shot. A shot pattern the size of a quarter became the standard for that rifle. It is very difficult to produce that kind of accuracy without tuning a load to your rifle.

If you don't have the time or the desire to load your own ammunition, a suitable alternative is to utilize the premium loads that are available from the ammunition makers. As I have gotten older and life has gotten busier, I began to do just that. I now shoot Federal Premium® 150 gr. Nosler Partition loads in my Browning® 7MM Rem magnum. It took trying a couple of the different loads Federal Premium makes, in my rifle, before I was able to determine which one would offer the best accuracy. I can produce a 1" pattern with my rifle, which I feel is adequate for my purposes. I suggest you do the same and find a load that is matched to your rifle through reloading or by testing various premium loads.

1. **OPTICS** The optics you utilize on your sheep hunt should be high quality optical equipment. Your rifle scope, rangefinder, spotting scope and binoculars should all be waterproof and work well in low-light conditions. They should all be as lightweight as possible, without sacrificing quality and clarity.

RIFLE SCOPE It's my belief that the most important features in a rifle scope are clarity, eye relief, and the ability to withstand recoil. I suggest before purchasing a scope, you check the clarity of it by picking out a point across the store and looking at it through the scope. Look through each of the scopes you are considering and compare what you see. You may be very surprised. I did this test a number of years ago between three quality scope manufacturers and was surprised to find that I could not see through one of the brands. I mentioned it to the clerk at the store and he indicated that he had the same problem. He said the brand in question used a coating on the lenses that was different than the other two. This is extremely important. If you cannot see through the scope in a lighted condition in the store, you surely won't be able to see through it at dawn or dusk in a low-light condition in the field. This could cost you a chance at filling your tag. Make sure you choose the scope that has the best clarity for the way you see.

You will also want a scope with long eye relief. Eye relief is the distance required between the scope lens and your eye for you to be able to see an object through the scope. You want the distance to be as long as possible to prevent the scope from striking your face when the rifle recoils at firing. You can check the manufacturer's specifications to learn what the eye relief is on the scope you are considering purchasing.

Finally, your scope should be built to withstand the recoil of your rifle, particularly if you shoot a magnum caliber. This seems like something that should be a given for a rifle scope, but not all scopes are created equal. You want a scope that is specifically made to withstand the effects of recoil over the life of the rifle scope. Again, you can check the manufacturer's specifications to confirm the scope you are considering purchasing will do just that.

I recommend your scope have a matte finish to minimize the possibility of it giving off glint in the bright sunlight. I prefer a variable power scope with a large objective size to gather as much light as possible in low-light situations. Choose the reticle style based on your personal preference. I prefer the duplex reticle. My personal preference for manufacturers has been Leupold®, but there are many other quality brand names available that will meet your needs.

BINOCULARS   Your binoculars are the second-most important piece of optical equipment you will utilize on your sheep hunt, behind your rifle scope. They will go with you everywhere you go on your hunt, so buy a "bino-system" harness to keep the weight of the binoculars off of your neck and on your shoulders.

I suggest a magnification of 8 or 10-power as it can be difficult to hold those of a larger magnification steady, particularly in the wind that you may experience above timberline. Make sure your binoculars have an armor-coating to protect them as well as dampen the noise they will make if they contact a hard surface. Work with your local sporting goods sales representative to choose the features that will best suit your needs and preferences. I have a pair of Swarovski® binoculars, as well as a pair of Zeiss® binoculars. Both are excellent in low light and have served me well, but again, there are many other quality brand names available that will meet your needs.

SPOTTING SCOPE   Item 2A on your list of important optical equipment will be your spotting scope. I suggest you buy a scope with as much magnification as you can afford. You will be looking at sheep at very long distances and the greater the magnification, the easier it will be to identify the game. Buy a quality tripod to match the weight of your scope.

The real challenge with choosing a spotting scope and tripod will be the dilemma you will face of weight vs. magnification. The greater the magnification, the larger the spotting scope. The larger the spotting scope, the larger the tripod will be needed. All of this will increase the weight you will be packing up and down the mountains. Use your best judgment.

My spotting scope is a Bausch & Lomb 20-50x60mm. I have a lightweight tripod I use with it. I bought it before my first sheep hunt and I chose it because it is fairly compact and I felt it would be easy to pack around.

RANGEFINDER   You will definitely want to have a rangefinder on your sheep hunt. It is designed to provide you with the distance to your quarry, but even more importantly, it will increase your confidence in making the shot and closing the deal.

Rangefinder technology has really made tremendous strides since the time I purchased my rangefinder before my first sheep hunt. The distance out to which they are accurate has increased, along with the development of features that can tell you the true ballistic distance to your quarry, when it is above or below you on the mountain. Another feature that I really like is the red readout, in lieu of the black LCD readout that is found in most units. Strides have also been made in making the units more compact.

My rangefinder is a Leica® and the reason I chose it was for the red readout, which at the time, was the only rangefinder on the market with such a readout. To me, it is far more readable under any light condition, and was worth the premium price I paid for it. Choose whatever unit you feel will work best for you, but make sure you bring a rangefinder along on your sheep hunt.

J.

PACKS AND PACK FRAMES   There are two types of packs to consider when planning for a sheep hunt, a daypack and a backpack. A daypack will allow you more freedom of movement and is less bulky, but if you kill a sheep, you will be making an extra trip out to get your pack frame in order to pack the animal out. A backpack will be more bulky, more restrictive to movement, and potentially noisier. But if you kill a sheep, you will be able to immediately pack a load of meat out.

DAYPACKS   There are two types of daypacks to consider, those you carry on your shoulders or those you carry on your waist. I prefer a waist pack, as I do not like carrying a load on my shoulders. Both types come in a variety of sizes and shapes and you can carry pretty much anything you might need for your hunt. One advantage of a shoulder pack is that many of today's models have integral water bladders. With a waist pack, you will have to utilize canteens to carry your water. As I stated earlier, the main disadvantage of carrying a daypack is that you will be hard-pressed to pack a quarter of meat out in it if you shoot a sheep. But a daypack is the way to go if you need to cover some ground and do it quietly.

BACKPACKS   There are two types of backpacks available, those with an internal frame and those with an external frame. I have no experience with an internal frame pack, so if you are interested in one, go to your local outdoor sporting goods store and talk to a sales associate. My backpack has an external frame. It is a Cabela's Alaskan Guide pack with frame and it is awesome! The pack is easily removed from the frame to allow for packing meat out. It is very heavy-duty with shoulder and waist straps that have thick padding. It is extremely comfortable and has served me well.

Whatever you do, go to the store and try on whichever type pack you are considering. You want to make sure it fits you well before you get out in the field on your hunt. Once you have purchased your pack, load it up with the equipment you will be carrying and go for a hike. If possible, put your pack frame to the test with 75 or 80 pounds of weight to simulate what it will be like to pack a quarter of meat on it. It will help you to improve your conditioning and give you a glimpse of how your pack will feel during the process of packing your animal out.

k.

HIKING GEAR During the course of a sheep hunt, you will be hiking and climbing in some of the most rugged country you have ever imagined. It will test your endurance. It will test your fitness. It will test your balance. And in some cases, it will test your courage.

WALKING STICKS To maximize all of these areas, I suggest you purchase and utilize walking sticks. Stoney Point® makes shooting sticks that can double as walking sticks. I have a pair that I bought before my second sheep hunt and they work great. The telescoping feature allows them to be extended for use or collapsed for carrying in your pack. They are equipped with rubber ends which, helps keep them quiet in the rocks of sheep country.

The importance of walking sticks, for your safety while walking and climbing, cannot be overstated. For you to safely navigate the steep, rocky terrain of sheep country, you should have three points of contact with the mountain at all times. That means both of your hands (via the walking stick) and one of your feet is touching the mountain at all times. This will help stabilize your balance and help prevent you from falling down the mountain.

I hunted without walking sticks during my first sheep hunt and ended up utilizing my rifle in some instances, as my walking stick, something I would not recommend. I purchased my walking sticks before my second sheep hunt and could not believe the difference it made in my balance and confidence as I hiked and climbed. I highly recommend that you get a pair of walking sticks and use them on your hunt.

FOAM SEATING PAD Another item that will make your hunt much more enjoyable is a foam seating pad. You will spend many hours during your sheep hunt sitting on the side of a mountain glassing through your binoculars or spotting scope, eating a meal or a snack, or just resting. A foam seating pad will make this activity much more bearable on the rocky ground of sheep country. My pad is made of approximately ¾ inch foam rubber that is about 14 inches square. It also has an elongated hand hole in it for easy carrying. It fits nicely into a daypack and is extremely lightweight. I put the saddle horn through the hand hole and used it as a saddle pad when I was riding horses during my second sheep hunt. It provided ample cushion to keep me from getting saddle sores and made riding horseback a lot more enjoyable. I highly recommend this item, also.

1. SURVIVAL GEAR

The last thing any hunter wants to do is end up in a survival situation. To date, I have never had to spend a night in the woods by myself. But if I did, I believe I have the know-how, and I carry the equipment necessary to allow me to do so.

During a sheep hunt, there are two primary reasons why you would find yourself in a survival situation...you are lost or you have injured yourself and cannot make it to safety on your own. In a survival situation, there are several things you need to be able to do. They include the ability to build a fire, build a shelter, treat your injuries (if you have them), and signal your rescuers.

FIRE STARTER Of primary importance in any survival situation is to be able to build a fire. To do so, you must have fuel and a means to create combustion. I carry waterproof matches in a waterproof container and cotton balls that have been rolled in petroleum jelly as the combustion material. I also carry them in a waterproof container (a plastic photographic film case works well). As a backup, I also carry a metallic fire starter made of magnesium. The unit has an integral scraper that can be used to scrape off shavings from the magnesium stick onto a pile of tinder. The scraper can then be quickly struck on the magnesium stick, creating sparks that will ignite the shavings and tinder. Kindling can then be added to get the fire going. You can then add larger sticks and logs for fuel.

The importance of building a fire in a survival situation cannot be understated. It will provide not only heat to keep you dry and warm, but also a psychological feeling of comfort during a very stressful time.

BUILD A SHELTER Weather conditions, and your location on the mountain, will have a great effect on your need for, and ability to build a shelter. Stormy conditions will increase your need to build a shelter. If you are above timberline when you find yourself in a survival situation, it will be much more difficult to build a shelter. You may have to seek shelter in a crevasse or cave if one is near. I carry a space blanket that is in the form of a sleeping bag for situations like this. You can crawl inside of it like a traditional sleeping bag and draw the opening closed around your neck to stay warm. This works much more effectively than a space blanket which can be unwieldy to use.

For shelter building, I carry enough lightweight rope to be able to lash a framework together for the shelter, or to tie between two trees to allow sticks to be leaned on it to create a tent-like structure. I carry a Leatherman® that has a knife that can be used to cut the rope. I also carry a bone saw in my pack that can be used to cut limbs and boughs for the shelter.

TREAT YOUR INJURIES   I carry a homemade first aid kit that includes Band-Aids and small bandages to treat cuts or scrapes. I have Advil® or aspirin for the relief of pain. Included in my kit is anti-diarrheal and Tums® for stomach problems and moleskin for blisters. I also carry an ace bandage and a small roll of trainers tape to aid in the treatment of sprained ankles. These items could also be used in conjunction with two sticks to create a splint for a broken limb. Finally, I also include a neoprene knee brace should I injure a knee. You will also want to include a couple of doses of any medications that you take.

SIGNAL YOUR RESCUERS   If you become lost or injured, you will want to be able to signal your rescuers. There are two ways to signal those who are coming to your rescue, audibly or visually. I carry a whistle that can be blown to signal audibly. It is far more efficient for you to blow a whistle than to yell or scream. The high pitch of the whistle will stand out from the other sounds of the forest and will carry further. You can also signal with your firearm by shooting three times in rapid succession and then pausing before firing three times again.

To be able to signal visually, I carry a small mirror. At night you can utilize your flashlight or head lamp. My headlamp has a flashing feature to help in drawing attention. I make sure I have spare batteries and bulbs to ensure my flashlight is in working condition. You can also utilize fire to signal your rescuers visually.

Finally, I recently downloaded an application for my smart phone called U.S. Army Survival. It is loaded with tips, instructions, and illustrations on how to survive in the wilderness. I encourage you to do the same before heading out on your hunt.

m.

ORIENTEERING   There are several items that are a must for navigating your way through sheep country. They include maps of your hunting area, a quality compass, and if possible, a GPS (global positioning system) device.

MAPS   Upon receiving notification that you have drawn a sheep tag, the first thing you should do is purchase topographical maps of the area you will be hunting. There are several options to consider including BLM maps, USGS topographical maps, and the book of topographical maps for the state in which you will be hunting which is published by Gazetteer. All of these can be found at the USGS (United States Geological Service) and many outdoor sporting goods stores. You can view the selection at your local USGS office or go to http://store.usgs.gov on the internet.

I usually buy the BLM map for the area I will be hunting along with the larger scale topographical maps offered by the USGS. I buy all of the USGS maps for the entire area I will be hunting. I get the overall layout of the area from the BLM map and the details of the area from the USGS maps. I mark the boundaries of my hunting area on both maps based on the written description found in the division of wildlife's hunting brochure. I fold the USGS maps and put both them and the BLM map in a Ziploc bag to keep them dry and carry them in my pack with me while I hunt.

COMPASS   I suggest you always have a compass with you whenever you are in the woods, whether hunting or not. To date, I have never had to use mine, but you never know. Your compass should be a quality instrument that includes a base plate, direction of travel arrow, movable degree dial, magnetic arrow, and orienteering arrow. This will allow you to set and read bearings in conjunction with your topographical maps. You can get such a compass from any quality outdoor sporting goods store, or go to the Scout Shop at your local Boy Scouts of America chapter. If you want to learn more about orienteering, you can also purchase the merit badge handbook for orienteering and study it. Doing so will help you to better understand how to use your compass and your maps.

GPS   For those of you who are more high-tech, you should consider purchasing a GPS device. With it, you can mark locations and map out routes into the field and back to your camp. You can mark a kill site, making it easier to return and pack out your animal. Depending upon the device, you can also download the topographical maps of your area to aid you in navigating throughout the area. If you do utilize a GPS, be sure to carry some spare batteries with you. Also, realize that the GPS will only operate if you can get a line of site between it, and at least two satellites.

INTUITION   Finally, unless you experience harsh weather or total darkness, you should be able to find your way back to safety utilizing good, old-fashioned intuition. I suggest while you are hunting, you constantly keep track in the back of your mind which way you must go to get back to your starting position, whether it be your ATV, your horse, or your camp. When possible, utilize landmarks (a mountain, a rock outcropping, a fence line, etc.) to help guide you.

I practice this, and in all of the years I have been hunting, I can think of only three times where I have been confused while in the field. In every case I wasn't lost, because I recognized the landmark at which I was looking. I just wasn't sure how it was that I had come to the point where I was looking at that landmark. After taking note of my location, I was then able to navigate my way back to my starting position.

Whatever you do, make sure you are proficient in the use of your orienteering equipment. Depending upon the situation, your safety and your life may depend upon it.

n.

COMMUNICATIONS EQUIPMENT   One of the greatest things about living in this day and age is the communications capability we enjoy. The technology we have is incredible, and it allows us to be connected no matter what we are doing, even sheep hunting. As you prepare for your sheep hunt, I suggest you plan to carry two out of the three following items, a cell/smart phone, a satellite phone, or a Spot® satellite GPS messenger.

CELL/SMART PHONES   While sheep hunting, you will definitely want to carry your cell phone and if you have a smart phone, even better. While cell coverage is generally spotty, it is still usually available. If you have a smart phone, they are usually equipped with a GPS, which is also a benefit. Both types of phones are equipped with a camera that makes it possible to send pictures to your friends and loved ones after you have harvested a sheep.

During my first sheep hunt, I carried my cell phone as a measure of comfort to my wife, since I was by myself during six of the nine days I hunted. Cell coverage was spotty but nevertheless available, and I was able to check in periodically. Carrying your cell phone is a must regardless if you have a companion on your hunt or not.

SATELLITE PHONES   Satellite phones are a type of mobile phone that communicate via a satellite system rather than terrestrial systems such as those utilized by cell phones. This makes satellite phones a more effective way to communicate from a remote location. If you will be hunting sheep in Canada or Alaska, a satellite phone will be a must for your safety. The newer models are about the same size as a smart phone, making them easy to carry in the field. They are somewhat pricey and are designed to be tied to a particular satellite system, so check with the supplier for coverage information. They can also be rented for about $40/week. You can check availability in your area on the internet. If you want greater communications reliability during your sheep hunt, you will want to have a satellite phone.

SPOT SATELLITE GPS MESSENGER   This device is incredible. It works in conjunction with the GPS satellite system and communicates your location to the network you designate, whether it be your home computer (via email), a cell phone (via text message), or the emergency response center. You can use it to check in with loved ones and friends. It will send your coordinates to them so that if you become lost or need help, you can easily be located. You can also allow others to track your adventure on-line and create a record of your locations for better future planning. If you get into trouble, you can notify your loved ones with the push of a button and they can call for help. Or if you have an emergency, you can push 911 and emergency rescue will be notified and sent to find you. You still have to be conscious to be able to push the button, but this device will improve the safety of your sheep hunt a hundredfold. I highly recommend this device, especially if you have to hunt solo on your own.

Spot also has a device (Spot Connect) that will work in conjunction with your smart phone to perform the same tracking and emergency functions. You can check them out online at www.findmespot.com.

CAMPING AND MISCELLANEOUS EQUIPMENT

O. During both of my sheep hunts, I hunted out of a base camp. Most of what I will discuss in this section will focus on the equipment needed to set up a base camp. If your desire is to backpack into the area you will be hunting, you will be using much the same equipment. However, it will need to be more compact, lightweight, able to fit into your backpack, and you will probably bring less equipment to cut down on weight.

TENTS If you hunt out of a base camp, I suggest you bring two tents, one to sleep in and one to cook in and house your supplies and gear. Chances will be very good that the country you will be camping in is bear country. By having a separate tent to sleep in, from where you cook and eat, you will lessen the possibility of being awakened by a bear attempting to enter the tent where you are sleeping. Be sure to bring a ground cloth for both of your tents to prevent the floors from getting wet in rainy weather.

SLEEPING GEAR If your tent is large enough, I strongly suggest you bring a cot to put your sleeping bag on. I sleep on a cot with a two inch foam pad and it makes sleeping much more restful. I usually bring two sleeping bags, one of which can serve as extra padding. If it's really cold, I put one inside the other for added warmth.

LANTERNS You will definitely want at least one lantern for light in your tent. I have the Coleman® propane lanterns that operate using the small canisters of propane. There are also kits available to allow them to utilize a larger propane tank. I love the fact that a propane lantern also provides a source of heat to take the chill off of the inside of your tent.

COOKING GEAR You will need a stove, at least one pot, one saucepan, and one skillet to cook in, along with some cooking utensils (large spoon, spatula, can opener, etc.) I have a 2-burner propane stove on which to do the bulk of my cooking. I also carry a single burner unit that can be used to heat water while I am cooking. If you go to REI, you can find cooking sets and utensils that will work well for base camp or a backpacking trip.

CUTLERY   Your cutlery needs to be fine quality steel that will hold an edge. You will utilize it around camp, as well as in the field while dressing your animal. Be sure to bring sharpening stones to sharpen your cutlery. You can find great compact knife sharpeners that can be carried in your pack that will work well no matter where you are. Check with your local outdoor sporting goods supplier for these units.

SAWS   You will want to bring a saw to cut firewood. You will also want to have a bone saw to aid in dressing your animal. It should easily fit in your backpack and needs to be lightweight.

MISCELLANEOUS EQUIPMENT   You will want to bring a small shovel with your gear. It will allow you to trench around your tent to divert water away from your sleeping quarters as well as serve as a snow shovel should the occasion arise. You can get a small shovel that collapses at your local Army/Navy Surplus store.

Be sure to bring a lighter to start your stove, lantern, and any other incendiary device.

Don't forget plates, cups and eating utensils. I generally bring paper and plastic for these items. They can be disposed of when you are through to cut down on the dishes you will have to do.

Make sure you bring a coffee pot to boil water with and to make coffee if you so desire. You will need tables for your cooking gear and on which to eat. I have two old folding tables that work well. I bring folding lawn chairs to sit on around camp. They double as clothes hangers and a place to put everything when I go to bed.

You will also need a wash basin. Mine is a plastic remnant from a hospital visit. Don't forget hand soap, dish soap, and washcloths and towels. I also bring several rolls of paper towels for multi-purpose use.

FLASHLIGHTS   You can never have too many flashlights when you are camping in the woods. I carry several compact units that can fit neatly into my backpack, as well as a couple of larger units for camp.

3. HYDRATION & NUTRITION

WATER & HYDRATION   One of the real challenges every hunter faces when hunting at high altitude is the potential to become dehydrated. The problem is the thin air. It contains less moisture. As a consequence, your body will naturally become dehydrated just by breathing. When you add that to the loss of body fluids caused by sweating as a result of hiking and climbing, you have the potential for nausea, additional fatigue, and leg cramps. The solution is to drink water, drink often, and drink a lot.   To do so, you have only two options…carry it or filter it.

CARRY IT   The drawback to carrying the necessary water that you will need is the weight of it. Sheep country is steep and high, and as I have stated numerous times, every pound you carry takes a toll on your body. The saving grace with carrying your water comes in the fact that every time you take a drink, you lighten your load by a few ounces.

Modern day ingenuity has brought us the water bladder, an excellent way to carry water. And with the integral sipping tube, you get the ability to hydrate while on the move. Many packs and day packs are equipped with bladders built right into them. As such, the weight of the water is distributed on your shoulders, thus easing the burden of carrying it.

There is also the old fashioned way of carrying water…in canteens. I actually prefer this method. I generally don't like having weight on my shoulders, so I carry a waste pack containing all of my gear, and it has built-in pouches for two canteens. Depending upon the air temperature during the day, and how much I exert myself, I can generally carry enough water in those two canteens to keep myself properly hydrated.

FILTER IT   A great way to supplement either method of carrying water is to carry a water filter. They are lightweight, compact, and simple to use. The challenge is you have to have a water source available to be able to use them. In sheep country, water is typically more plentiful near the base of the mountains. It can also be found in the small creeks that run down the mountain sides. But when you get above timberline, where you will spend much of your time sheep hunting, water sources can be hard to find. It is for this reason that I recommend you refrain from only carrying a filter to take care of your clean water needs.

I carry a water bottle that has an integral filter inside of it. I carry the bottle empty to minimize the weight. If I drink my canteens dry, I fill the bottle with water from a creek or spring, and as I suck on the straw that is integral to the filter, the water is pulled through the filter and cleansed before reaching my mouth. It works great and I highly recommend this type of filtering system. You can find them at any quality outdoor sporting goods store. Whatever you do, be sure to check your maps of the area in advance of heading into the field to know where the potential water sources are, should you have the need to use your filter.

Finally, a word to the wise about drinking unfiltered water. Before purchasing my water filter, there were a couple of occasions where I ran out of water during a hunt and had to drink unfiltered stream water. I did so without any negative repercussions, but I do not recommend it. Mountain streams most often contain parasites and bacteria that can wreak havoc with your intestinal tract and make you miserable and possibly end your hunt. Be wise and carry some kind of water filter along on your hunt.

q. **FOOD** As stated earlier, sheep hunting is extremely strenuous and a hunter can burn up to 7000 calories a day. In order to remain at peak efficiency, you must have enough caloric intake with the proper nutritional value and the necessary protein, to rebuild muscle and maintain your energy level. You will also need to consider the weight, bulk, and packaging of the food you will be consuming on your hunt. If you will be backpacking during your hunt, you will want to consider the amount of water needed to cook your food. And finally, the palatability of your food will play a major part in your calorie intake. If it doesn't taste good, you probably won't eat it. Be sure to take foods you enjoy and test those you have not previously eaten prior to your hunt. When planning your food, I suggest you break it into two categories, meals and snacks.

MEALS When it comes to meals, one of my main concerns involves ease of preparation. I usually have instant oatmeal and a banana for breakfast, along with some juice or milk. For lunch, I bring lunchmeat, whole grain bread, and cheese slices for sandwiches. I also bring carrots, celery sticks, block cheese, and fruit or fruit cups to round out the items for lunch. For evening meals, after a long day of hunting, the last thing you want to do is spend a lot of time preparing your food. If you will be hunting out of a base camp, I suggest you bring items that have been previously prepared. I often bring chili and stew which has been prepared at home and frozen. These items will thaw during the course of your hunt while stored in your cooler and can be quickly warmed for a hot and satisfying meal. Add a few crackers, or a loaf of bread, and a can of fruit to round out the meal. I also like sloppy joes for a quick and easy meal. Brown some hamburger and add the sloppy joe mix (powdered or canned), add buns and you have a meal you can prepare in less than 15 minutes. All of these dinner items can be heated in one pan, making cleanup quick and easy.

I also bring a jar of peanut butter and a jar of jelly and some extra bread, along with several packages of ramen noodles as backup, should my hunt run long.

If you plan to do any backpacking during your hunt, I suggest a trip to your local outdoor sporting goods store to purchase some freeze-dried meals. If you have never eaten them, be sure you try them before go on your hunt. Most of them are very tasty, but I've had a few that were not good. You don't want to be somewhere in the wilderness and discover that the food you brought is inedible.

SNACKS   My snacks include jerky and sunflower seeds for salt replenishment. I bring dried fruit, trail mix, apples, granola bars, and nutritional bars for nourishment and a variety of miniature candy bars for energy. I pack these items in Ziploc® bags in quantities sufficient to get me through the day.

DRINK   I bring milk and orange or grape juice for breakfast. I bring box juices or the small, individual size sports drinks to carry in my pack for lunch and breaks. For dinner I bring some kind of juice high in potassium to help fight leg cramps. I refrain from drinking caffeinated drinks during my hunts because caffeine acts as a diuretic, which can contribute to dehydration.

SUPPLEMENTS AND VITAMINS   I take a variety of supplements and vitamins on a daily basis and my hunting trips are no different. It is difficult to replenish all of the nutrients you burn during a sheep hunt and taking supplements and vitamins helps ensure your body is getting what it needs to stay at peak performance. Finally, my recommendations may not suit your tastes. Make sure you bring the food and drink that you enjoy and plan for sufficient quantities necessary to make it through your hunt.

4. SHEEP STEW

r. **MISCELLANEOUS SUGGESTIONS AND IDEAS** Here are a few miscellaneous suggestions to help you in your preparation for your hunt and during your hunt.

SAFETY Sheep country is some of the most rugged, remote country you will ever hunt. You will deal with steep slopes, loose rocks, and a variety of weather conditions that can increase your risk for injury. Safety must be at the forefront of your thoughts as you hunt. I strongly recommend that you make sure to have at least one partner to hunt with you.

Thunderstorms are a real possibility during the early portion of the season. Believe me, there is nothing more nerve racking than lightning cracking around you while hunting above timberline. Should you get caught in a thunderstorm in an area where there is no cover, I suggest you put your rifle down and get some distance away from it. Look for large rocks that you can crouch near or a crevasse or cave that you might crawl into. Lower your profile as much as possible to lessen the possibility of getting struck by lightning.

PREVENTING LEG CRAMPS I have poor circulation in my legs which makes dealing with leg cramps almost a given when I hike a significant amount. I've learned that there are a couple of things I can do to help prevent them from occurring. Prevention, for me, begins with eating a banana every morning prior to heading into the field. During the day while hunting, I drink a lot of water. I also carry a bottle of sports drink that I consume while hunting. After returning to camp, I drink at least 8 ounces of some kind of juice that is high in potassium. Before I retire to bed at the end of the day, I spend at least five minutes doing various stretching exercises. At some point in the evening, I also lie down and put my legs up above the level of my heart for ten minutes. This has proven to be one of the best things I do to aid in the prevention of leg cramps. It can also be done in the field while taking a break.

BUY QUALITY   Sheep hunting is one hunt that will test the quality of your equipment. If you can afford to do so, make sure you don't scrimp on quality. It's been my experience that you definitely get what you pay for.   I have never been disappointed when I have bought quality equipment. That doesn't mean you cannot get a deal on your quality equipment. In the back of every Cabela's is an area called The Bargain Cave. There you can find some great deals on a host of different equipment that you will need on your hunt. I found my Swarovski® binoculars and Leica® rangefinder before my first sheep hunt. Both items were returns from a previous customer and both items were in perfect condition. Do your homework and look for the deals. They're out there.

JOURNAL YOUR EXPERIENCE   To preserve this wonderful experience that will be your sheep hunt, I suggest you journal it. Begin by taking lots of pictures, starting with the packing of your vehicle. Continue to take pictures throughout the trip. Buy a small journal and keep an accounting of the occurrences of each day. At the conclusion of the hunt, write a short story of the adventure. Magazines like Eastman's Journal and The Huntin'Fool depend upon stories from hunters like you and me to fill the pages of their publications. I had the story of my second sheep published in the December, 2006 edition of The Huntin'Fool and it was exciting. It will be exciting for you too if you are lucky enough to harvest a sheep and get your story published. Do not worry if you're not the greatest writer, you can get a friend to help you put the story together. Realize also, that every hunting magazine employs editors that can polish your story, if need be. Take the time to do this. It will help you to relive your hunt for years to come.

5. PRE-HUNT

S. **PRE-SEASON ACTIVITES** Determining the location of the sheep in your hunting area should begin long before your season starts. There is significant information available that will help you, as a sheep hunter, to become successful. It will take time and research to find it. But doing so will help you to know where to best do your pre-season scouting.

RESEARCH Locating the sheep begins with research. I suggest you start with a call to the biologist who oversees the area in the state you will be hunting. They typically work for the state game and fish department. You can get the biologist's phone number on the department's website. I contacted the Colorado Division of Wildlife's biologist prior to my first sheep hunt and was pleasantly surprised at how helpful she was. She gave me great information and I could tell she truly wanted me to have a successful hunt. Since I lived in the state I was going to hunt in, I also made a trip down to the DOW's offices and researched the harvest data from previous years. Successful sheep hunters are required to provide information as to the location they killed their animal and this information is open to public review. (I later learned that those records are only about 20% accurate.) So while it was an entertaining couple of hours of research, the kill site information wasn't much good. What I did learn though, that was extremely worthwhile, was the names of the hunters who had previously hunted in my area. Many of them listed their phone numbers and I was able to call and learn directly from them about their sheep hunting experience in the area. That information was invaluable to me in deciding where to begin my scouting efforts.

PRE-SEASON SCOUTING I cannot stress enough how important pre-season scouting will be to your potential success in harvesting a sheep. Pre-season scouting will not guarantee your success, but failing to scout will most assuredly reduce your chances for success. Pre-season scouting will not only help you to locate the animals in the area, it will also help you to become familiar with the terrain and the easiest ways to access the area. Learning the easiest access routes will help to reduce the physical strain you experience during the hunt.

When scouting, the best way to spot animals is to first get as high up on the ridge as possible across from where you will be hunting, then to sit down and begin glassing with your binoculars. Once you find an animal, you can then look at it through your spotting scope to identify its gender, horn size, etc. I systematically look at every inch of the terrain I see in the field of view in my binoculars. I do so by moving my eyes and not the binoculars. I look for light-colored spots, similar to the color of the animal that I am pursuing. I also look for white spots on the side of the hill. This could be a rump patch on an animal. I also look for shadows that could be cast by a feeding animal. While I am looking for color variations and shadows, I am also looking for any movement I might see. Once I have thoroughly covered an area on the side of the hill, I move my binoculars to the next area and begin the process over again. Realize that this process is not fool-proof. During my first sheep hunt, I sat for several hours looking at the side of a hill only to have a whole herd of sheep stand up and begin feeding in an area where I thought I had thoroughly studied. Sheep blend in well with their surroundings and even your best effort will sometimes come up short.

If you have difficulty finding animals through your binoculars, you can also glass through your spotting scope. I have found many an animal by utilizing this technique. To reduce eye strain, I suggest you purchase an eye patch and place it over the eye you are not using to look through the spotting scope. Aim the spotting scope at an area on the mountain and then move your eye to look at every inch of the view, again searching for color, shadows, or movement.

Be patient when scouting. Prior to my first sheep hunt, my pre-season scouting efforts took me to my area on nine different days before I even spotted a sheep. When I went back the tenth day, they were in the same location as the time before. Guess where I hunted on opening day? That's correct...right where I saw the sheep during my pre-season scouting. Guess where every encounter I had with a sheep occurred during that first hunt? You guessed it again...right where I saw the sheep during my pre-season scouting.

What if you don't happen to live in the state where you will be sheep hunting? Then I suggest that you plan your hunt to arrive a couple of days prior to the beginning of the season. Spend those extra days in the field scouting for animals. Do your research as outlined previously so you will know the locations you most likely will be able to find sheep. In addition, talk to the local game warden and residents to help you verify your research and determine where sheep have been spotted recently. It won't be ideal, but it will improve your chances of success and every little bit you do will help.

6. THE HUNT

LOCATING THE SHEEP   You can expect that a significant portion of your sheep hunt will be spent looking for sheep.   This is where your pre-season research and scouting efforts will pay off.   It is one of the things that make sheep hunting such a favorite of mine. As one of my sheep hunter friends says, "Sheep hunting isn't just a 'drive by shooting' like much of what we do when we go big game hunting."   Sheep hunting truly is hunting in the purest sense.

Sheep live in difficult terrain. It's high, it's steep, it's rocky and it's expansive. Hiking around your hunting area to find the animals will do nothing but waste a lot of precious time and energy. It is best to first locate them utilizing the same methods used in your pre-season scouting.

As I compared my first sheep hunt to my second, I concluded that I did far too much hiking vs. locating sheep in my first hunt. I saw a lot of the area first hand, but it wore me out physically. During my second hunt I spent much more time glassing for sheep, and as it turned out, I ended up filling my tag.

Do yourself a favor, and save your legs by placing a priority on utilizing your binoculars and spotting scope.

u. **THE STALK** You've spotted a ram. He's a legal ram and he meets the criteria you set for yourself for size of horns and length of curl. The stalk begins! As with any big game animal, sheep have great noses, so take special care to stay downwind from him. I carry a bottle of "wind checker" with me when I am hunting, which is nothing more than a small plastic squeeze bottle filled with an odorless powder that is released into the air when the bottle is squeezed. It makes it very easy to check the direction of the wind. Make sure you account for the thermals that occur naturally when hunting in the mountains. In the morning hours, the thermals blow down the mountain, and in the afternoon and evening, they blow up the mountain. Also be aware that the winds tend to swirl in the mountains, so check the wind direction often.

Prior to beginning the stalk, find a landmark by which you can guide yourself. You should strive to stay out of site as much as possible and using a landmark will help to keep you on course. Take a visual of the animal as often as possible to help save steps. Stop often and take notice of everything that is around you.

Do your best to make sure you take your time during the stalk. Even if you have a great distance to go to get into position to take a shot, you must take care to not rush. There may be other game species in the area, such as mule deer or elk that could spook and blow the stalk. I had this happen to me during a stalk on my second sheep hunt. We knew there was a herd of elk just to the north of where the ram was that we were after, and we thought we were far enough to the south not to spook them. We thought we had the wind figured out, but it swirled on us and the elk caught our scent and stampeded right at the ram. One of the guides who stayed down below at the truck later related to us that it was almost comical how the ram had to scramble to keep from being trampled by the thirty or so elk that were in the herd. Needless to say, I did not get a shot at the ram.

If possible, try to approach your sheep from a position that is even, or slightly higher in elevation, than the position of the animal. As I stated earlier, they rarely look up, so coming in on them from a position that is higher than theirs will be to your advantage.

44

Use your rangefinder to keep track of the distance to your prey. Get as close as possible, but once you are inside the range of where you believe you can comfortably make the shot (and you should have a feel from this through the practice that you did prior to the hunt or through previous hunting experience), take care not to get too greedy by trying to get too close. You may have just walked several miles with hundreds or even several thousands of feet of elevation change. Save yourself the disappointment of blowing the stalk and have the confidence in yourself to take the shot!

V.

MAKING THE SHOT   It's the moment of truth. You've hiked your legs off to get into position to be able to take a shot at this ram. Because you've read this book, you've taken my advice and spent time during your hunt as you have been hiking, thinking about your reactions when the time would come to make the shot. Your mind is focused. Your rifle is on a rest or your shooting sticks. You are in a position that is comfortable for you to be able to make the shot. Your scope is dialed in. You've put a shell in the chamber, the safety is off and you have the animal in your sites. You are waiting for him to turn to where you can hit his vitals, and in the process, break his opposite shoulder so that no matter what, he is not going anywhere once your bullet hits him. Your breathing is controlled. You're relaxed. He's moved into the position you have been waiting for. You take a breath and as you exhale, you squeeze the trigger. Boom! The rifle goes off and down he goes! You've just shot your first bighorn sheep! The celebration can begin! A rush of excitement combined with relief pours over you. It's hard to believe you have accomplished your goal of harvesting a sheep. What a moment!

I've just described the perfect scenario for taking a bighorn sheep. Guess what? It's probably not going to go down this way. Here's what happened to me on my second sheep hunt.

It was the moment of truth. It was the last day of my hunt and there was about 45 minutes left before the sun would be down. My guide and I had hiked our legs off to get into position to be able to take a shot at this ram. I had spent time as I was hiking, thinking about what my reactions when the time came to make the shot. My mind was focused. My rifle was on my shooting sticks. I was in a position that was comfortable for me to be able to make the shot. My scope was dialed in. I had put a shell in the chamber, the safety was off and I had the animal in my sites. We had taken a position that was above him and my guide whispered to aim low. I was confident he was not going to go anywhere once my bullet hit him. My breathing was controlled. I relaxed. I took a breath and as I exhaled, I squeezed the trigger. Click! My rifle misfired! In twenty plus years of hunting with that rifle it had never misfired. And now with the most important shot I had ever taken at a big game animal on the line, it misfired. Fortunately, I was able to eject the shell and chamber another one. By now, both my guide and I were worried that the wind would swirl and he would be gone. I put the sites on him again and squeezed the trigger. Boom! Not only did he not go down, he started to run to the right towards the edge of the ridge. In my mind I was thinking, "You have got to be kidding me! I have hiked my guts out and when I finally get a chance to take a shot, I missed!" I jacked another shell into the chamber and just as the ram reached the edge of the ridge, he slowed to a walk and I fired again. The shot locked him up and he began to tumble down the mountain. I exhaled and laid back onto the side of the mountain as a rush of excitement combined with a feeling of relief poured over me. "Nice shot, Bill!" my guide exclaimed and the celebrating began. It was the last shell in my rifle, 45 minutes before sundown on the last day of my hunt. It wasn't pretty, but it worked. It was hard to believe I had accomplished my goal of harvesting a sheep. What a moment!

The moral of the story…prepare yourself. You never know what will happen. Be ready to react.

PICTURE TIME! You've done it! Your ram is on the ground and its picture time! Taking a bighorn sheep is a unique and precious achievement, something that few hunters have accomplished. You will want to memorialize the occasion with as many pictures as possible. Not only do the pictures need to capture the moment, they need to be tastefully done.

Start by cleaning the blood off of the animal, in particular, his face. Because sheep live in such steep country, it's not uncommon for the animal to roll several hundred feet down the mountainside after being shot. This often leaves them bleeding from the mouth and the nose. Make sure you have plenty of rags in your daypack to clean the blood off of your kill. Use some water from your canteen to help in the process. Keep wiping and using fresh rags until your animal is clean. This applies to the animal's body, also.

Next, determine how you want to pose yourself and the animal for the pictures. Depending upon where your animal has fallen, it may be difficult to set up for the pictures at the kill site. If you have help, and there is a location nearby where you could move the animal to better pose it and yourself, you should do so. Take the time to do it right, you will be glad you did.

Earlier, I encouraged you to create a scrapbook of pictures to help you become familiar with how to field judge sheep. Utilize what you saw in those pictures to help you determine how to set up for your pictures. If you have a hunting companion with you, have them take the pictures, but check each picture after it has been taken to make sure they have framed the picture correctly, that your face is not in a shadow, and that the subject is close enough. Look at the details of the picture. Is the animal's tongue hanging out? Is your face contorted or are you smiling? Are your eyes open? This is very important. You only get one chance to take these pictures correctly and you want to make sure you are satisfied with them. Believe me, just because someone can hold a camera and press the shudder button does not mean they know how to take pictures. I have experienced the regret that comes from not taking the time to make sure I was happy with my pictures.

Use a high megapixel camera. This is especially important if you plan on submitting the pictures for publication in a hunting magazine. If your camera does not have high enough resolution, the magazine may not be able to publish your pictures.

Make sure you zoom in close enough. This is extremely important. Fill the frame with you and the animal. It makes the picture so much more vivid and alive. Use your flash, even if the sun is out. It will get rid of the shadows on your face.

If for whatever reason, you do not have anyone with you to take the pictures, never fear, you can do it yourself. I carry a miniature tripod that is about 4" high with me in my waste pack that I have utilized on several occasions to take pictures by myself. You can do it by using the timer feature on the camera, setting the timer, and then hustling to get into position and posed before the timer goes off and the shudder fires. It may take a few times to get a shot correct, but it works!

Finally, I read an article by Guy Eastman, publisher of The Eastman's Hunting Journal a while back regarding how to take hunting pictures. You would be well served to look it up on their website at www.eastmans.com as part of your preparation for your hunt.

X.

THE REAL WORK BEGINS The pictures have been taken and the celebration has subsided. The time has come for the real work to begin. You must now cape, skin, quarter, and debone the animal so he can be packed off of the mountain.

CAPING Properly removing the cape of the animal is the most important thing you will do if you plan to have the head mounted. You want to provide ample hide for your taxidermist to ensure that he will be able to create a beautiful mount. To do so, begin by splitting the hide at the midway point between the front and hind legs completely around the torso of the animal. It is easiest to use a knife with a gut-hook to do this, but it can also be done with any skinning knife. My outfitter actually used a seatbelt cutter to accomplish this while caping the sheep I harvested on my second hunt. It worked so slick that I purchased one, and have used it on a couple of animals that I have taken since my sheep hunt.

Once you have the hide split completely around the animal, split the hide up the backbone to a point between the ears. Then carefully skin the animal working from the back, forwards towards the head. When you come to the front legs, split the hide down the inside of both legs to the knee joints. Cut the hide completely around the knee joints and skin both legs, leaving the hide in tact where it meets the body of the sheep. Do your best to take as much care as possible to not cut through the hide as you skin the cape. Small holes in the cape can be repaired by your taxidermist, but strive to minimize the number that you make. Once you have skinned the cape to the base of the jawbone, take a bone saw and cut the head off of the neck of the animal.

I suggest you leave skinning the head to your taxidermist. You really want to minimize any holes in that section of the cape, so unless you completely know what you are doing, leave that for the experts.

SKINNING & QUARTERING When you are finished with removing the cape and head, you are now ready to complete the skinning and quartering of the animal. If you plan to retain the remainder of the hide, split it along the center of the belly all the way to the anus. You can then repeat the procedure you followed with the front legs on the hind legs by cutting around the knee joints of both legs and then splitting the hide on the inside of both legs down to the cut at the belly. Skin the carcass to a point just past the back bone. You can now remove the front and hind quarters that have been exposed, along with the backstrap on that side of the animal. As you remove each quarter or backstrap, place it in a game bag to keep it clean and lay it aside. Before rolling the animal over to complete the process on the other side, make an 8-10 inch slit in the meat behind the ribs near the backbone. This will expose the loin and will allow you to reach into the cavity of the animal with your hand and knife to peel the loin away from the backbone. Once you have removed the loin, roll the carcass over and repeat the same process to finish skinning and quartering the animal.

DEBONING If you will have to pack your animal more than 200 yards, I strongly suggest that you de-bone the meat. The bones of any animal are the bulk of the weight and leaving them in the meat serves no purpose. It only takes a few minutes and the weight you will save by doing so will be worth every second of time you take to do it.

To do so, remove one of the quarters from the game bag and place the quarter on the fleshy side of the hide. Feel where the bone is in the quarter and make a cut through the meat to the bone. Then as you pull the meat away from the bone, keep cutting along the bone to allow the meat to peel off of it. When you are through removing the bone, place the meat back in the game bag and seal it up for packing. Repeat the process with all four quarters.

You are now ready to pack the meat out. Notice that nowhere in this process did you open the cavity of the animal to gut it. It's not necessary unless you plan to keep the heart or the liver, which I don't care for, and which most generally has been destroyed by your bullet anyway. I learned this process from the outfitter who dressed my sheep after I harvested it, and I find it to be so much easier and less messy than gutting the animal. Try it. You'll never go back to gutting your big game animals.

PACKING OUT   Of all the things you must do after you kill an animal, this is the most exhausting. Unless you have hunted with an outfitter who has horses or mules, you get to be the pack animal. Begin by securing the meat to your pack frame. There are three methods available to secure the meat to your pack frame. They are rope, bungee cords, or rubber bungees. I generally use rope rather than the other two methods. Rope can be cinched down much tighter than bungee cords. While rubber bungees will secure the meat about as well as rope, they are far heavier to carry in your pack. You want to ensure that the meat is secured as tightly as possible to prevent it from shifting on your pack and possibly causing you to lose your balance and fall down the mountain during the hike out.

Know your capabilities regarding how much weight you will be able to pack. I suggest you learn your capability prior to your hunt by tying various amounts of weight on your pack frame and carrying it during your training regimen. While you won't have a scale in the field to verify the amount of weight you are about to carry, you will at least have a feel for what you will be comfortable carrying. Remember, sheep country is steep and rocky and navigating it without an extra 75 pounds on your back is difficult enough, so be prudent when deciding how much weight to tie onto your pack. At the same time, realize that you want to take as few trips as possible to get your animal packed out. It will be during the process of packing out that you will come to understand the money you spent to purchase walking sticks was worth every penny that left your wallet.

7. POST-HUNT

Y. **CARING FOR YOUR TROPHY AND MEAT** You have just taken one of the finest big game animals in all of the world. In order to ensure the quality of both the mount and the meat, you must take special care of them. Here are some suggestions.

CARING FOR THE MEAT There are a few basic rules you will want to follow to ensure the quality of the meat you have harvested. To me, sheep meat is the finest game meat available and you will want to make sure it remains as clean as possible prior to delivering it to your butcher. Use quality game bags that are heavy enough not to tear from the weight of the meat. Keep the meat out of the sunlight as much as possible. Once you have returned to camp, hang the meat far enough off of the ground as possible to protect it from predators such as coyotes, wolves or bears. Hanging the meat will also allow it to cool as much as possible.

Transport the meat to your butcher as quickly as possible. If you have to travel a significant distance to your meat processor (several days or more), you might want to consider utilizing the services of a local big game butcher who can then ship the meat to your home once it has been processed and frozen. Talk to the local residents, hunters, and outfitters to see who they recommend. If you're like me and live in the state where you hunted, wrap the meat in a tarp if you will be transporting it on an open-air trailer. This will ensure it stays clean from road dust or splash-back. You can also transport the meat in plastic containers or coolers. If you put ice in the containers, take care to make sure the meat does not get wet. I much prefer the tarp method as it allows the meat to breathe better vs. an enclosed container.

CARING FOR YOUR TROPHY You will want the cape of your sheep to cool just like the meat. You will also want to protect it from predators just like the meat. If it is going to be more than a few days before you deliver the cape and hide to your taxidermist, you will want to salt and flesh the hide. This will help to dry the hide and keep the hair from slipping. Talk to a local taxidermist to learn how to do this prior to your hunt.

CHOOSING A TAXIDERMIST One of the most important decisions you will make after your hunt is which taxidermist you will select to mount your trophy. There are many taxidermists and few artists. Considering the amount of money that will be spent and the work that will be done to harvest a sheep, this decision should be made carefully. I suggest you contact several taxidermists and make a visit to their shops to view their work. In addition, seek recommendations from past customers. This will help to make your decision-making process easier. Choose your taxidermist based on the quality of his work and your feelings as to his ability to re-create the image of your trophy, not the fees that you will be charged. You only get one chance to get this right so do your homework and choose wisely.

COMPLETING STATE REGULATIONS Most every state has regulations that must be completed within a certain timeframe after you harvest a sheep. They generally include an inspection of the head, drilling the horns and inserting an identification plug, recording the location of the kill, and obtaining other items of information regarding the animal. Be aware and make sure you complete the requirement during the timeframe allotted. Failure to do so could involve fines and other penalties.

Z. **WHAT NOW?** You've just taken your first bighorn sheep, what now? If you're like me you've contracted sheep fever and you can't wait until your next opportunity to go sheep hunting. Unless you have a lot of money and are able to buy a governor's tag or one of The Wild Sheep Foundation's auction tags, it could be a while until your next hunt. So how do you deal with this unbearable itch you have to sheep hunt? I have several suggestions.

APPLYING FOR TAGS IN OTHER STATES As Garth Carter of Carter Hunter Services suggests, Apply, Apply, Apply! Every western state has bighorn sheep and the only way to get a tag is to apply. I suggest obtaining a subscription to "The Huntin'Fool," the hunting publication from Carter Hunter Services. They provide information on sheep hunting in every western state including the application deadlines, the costs to apply, specific harvest data and odds of drawing in each hunt area, and much, much more. The cost is $100 annually to be a member and it will be the best $100 you spend each year. The magazine is first class and is published monthly. I'm convinced the reason I was able to draw two sheep tags within a twelve year period was because of the information I was able to utilize from "The Huntin'Fool." Join, you'll be glad you did.

APPLY FOR RAFFLE TAGS How lucky are you? Well, if you bought this book, you probably drew a sheep tag. And, if you consider the odds you faced to draw that tag, it's as if you won the lottery. So with that in mind, you should consider purchasing chances on the raffle tags that most every western state offers. These tags are given to the various conservation organizations such as The Wild Sheep Foundation, Rocky Mountain Elk Foundation, Mule Deer Foundation, etc. to raise money to fund their conservation efforts. The raffle tickets are priced in the $25 to $100 range, so if you purchase one ticket and your name is picked, you have a great opportunity to hunt for a really great price. I buy several raffle tickets every year. I haven't won a tag yet, but you never know. Remember, you can't win if you don't buy a ticket.

ATTEND A SHEEP SHOW   Every year during the first few months of the year, there are incredible hunting expositions held in various locations around the country. I encourage you to select at least one of the shows provided by either The Wild Sheep Foundation or the Grand Slam Club and attend. You will see fantastic exhibits, meet outfitters and equipment manufacturers, and enjoy an experience that can best be described as sheep hunting nirvana. Unless you live in the state where these shows are held (usually Nevada), you will have to travel to get to them, but believe me, the time and money will be well spent. You will not go home disappointed if you attend!

VOLUNTEER   I encourage you to join either The Wild Sheep Foundation or the Grand Slam Club. Both of these organizations are committed to improving sheep habitat and helping wild sheep to thrive. Through them, you can volunteer to help with projects that will improve habitat and promote the well-being of wild sheep. Similar projects are conducted by many of the state wildlife departments and you can volunteer with them also. Prior to my first sheep hunt, I volunteered with the Colorado Division of Wildlife to help with their annual sheep and goat count in the hunting area in which I had drawn a tag. Doing so allowed me to better get to know the local DOW biologist for the area, as well as to hike and scout the area. I only saw one ram during the two days that we hiked, but I saw dozens of mule deer bucks (some of them shooters!), hundreds of elk, and even a few mountain goats.

COMPANY/PRODUCT ENDORSEMENTS

Below is a list of companies and products that I have used and endorse. I encourage you to check them out.

SPORTING GOODS RETAILERS

Cabela's www.cabelas.com

Bass Pro Shops www.basspro.com

Sportsman's Warehouse www.sportsmanswarehouse.com

RIFLES

Browning Rifles www.browning.com

AMMUNITION

Federal Premium Ammunition www.federalpremium.com

Nosler Bullets www.nosler.com

CLOTHING

Browning Sporting Goods Co. www.browning.com

Columbia Sportswear www.columbia.com

FOOTWEAR

Rocky Boots www.rockyboots.com

OPTICS

Leupold Rifle Scopes www.leupold.com

Swarovski Optik www.swarovskioptik.com

Zeiss Binoculars www.zeiss.com

Leica Rangefinders www.leica.com

GPS SAFETY SYSTEMS

Spot Satellite GPS www.findmespot.com

Garmin GPS www.garmin.com

CUTLERY

Knives www.gerbergear.com

Leatherman Tool www.leatherman.com

CAMPING

Tents and Camping Equipment www.rei.com

Outfitters Tent and Stove www.davistent.com

MISCELLANEOUS

Stoney Point Shooting Sticks www.stoneypoint.com

OUTFITTERS

Horn Fork Guides www.coloradobiggameoutfitter.com

SUMMARY

Well there you have it. I hope you enjoyed reading this book as much as I enjoyed writing it. This endeavor allowed me to again experience both of my sheep hunts over the period of several months, and I have to tell you it was exhilarating! There is nothing in the world like sheep hunting, and it's my hope that your first sheep hunt will plant in your heart an enthusiasm for the sport that will never die. I wish you the very best in your pursuit of that "ram of a lifetime!"

Made in the USA
Lexington, KY
30 July 2013